Speck *of* Dust

Speck *of* Dust

Collection of Short Poems

HAMID MOJDEHI

RESOURCE *Publications* · Eugene, Oregon

SPECK OF DUST
Collection of Short Poems

Resource Publications
An Imprint of Wipf and Stock Publishers
199 W. 8th Ave., Suite 3
Eugene, OR 97401

www.wipfandstock.com

PAPERBACK ISBN: 978-1-6667-4316-6
HARDCOVER ISBN: 978-1-6667-4317-3
EBOOK ISBN: 978-1-6667-4318-0

MAY 10, 2022 10:01 AM

This book is dedicated to my family and to all those who live curiously intrigued by life and role of Man in it.

CONTENTS

PREFACE

T HIS book is a collection of short poems written in the qua-
train format and inspired by the poems of the ancient Per-
sian poet Omar Khayyam. Each poem is easy to understand while
at the same time carries a deeper philosophical theme. They touch
on various aspects of Man's life such as life itself as we know it,
love, hope and our final departure from this world into oblivion. If
you enjoy rhyming poetry that excites your senses and at the same
time makes you wonder about the unanswered puzzles of life and
Man's role in it, then you'll find this book an enjoyable read.

GLARE OF LIFE

in a desert there are no flowers around
in a freezing cold there are no blossoms to be found
within us sometimes parched deserts or wild cold storms abound
but once you let in joy, the glares of life astound

FLEETING LIFE

see the blue sky and the sun like a diamond in its belly
see the flowers and the butterflies dancing around them so silly
I am still drowned in thoughts of things I missed to do yesterday
   or want to do tomorrow
unaware of how this fleeting life will pass me by in a flick of a
   penny

DREAM

saw you in a dream coming towards me from a distance
I ran to you, embraced you and kissed you all over with
    persistence
you smiled at me so softly, as you always did in life
you looked at me as if to say, appreciate fully your one-time realm
    of existence

LITTLE KIDS

asked a wise man please let me know
who is the best teacher of Man to help him shine and glow?
he said calmly with no hesitation at all
the best teachers in life are the little kids around you, watch them
   closely, specially when they are putting on a show

YOUR SMILE

O' my little one, put your head on my shoulder
those tear drops you shed crush me hard like a boulder
when you smile all sorrow disappears from my heart
when you laugh, my world lights up and I too become a kid,
  much bolder

MOUNTAIN OF GOLD

early in the morning along came a little baby into the world
with him the world of a man and a woman changed, as if given a
   new mold
though the baby is so tiny and so frail
his existence is as powerful as an earthquake and he is as precious
   as a mountain of gold

LIFE'S SYMPHONY

When what I do and my true feelings inside are in harmony
I will be like a child, pure and simple, enjoying life without
tyranny
how I wish this journey of life could continue in peace
could gently go with the flow of life, riding the waves graciously,
listening to life's symphony

PARADOX OF MAN

asked a wise man who he would consider as insane?
he replied the one who doesn't know where he has come from
    and where he is going, while always in pain
I asked, aren't we all insane then my great man of wonder?
he smiled and whispered softly; this is the paradox of Man, I
    must say in shame

STOLEN HEART

in a day like today, a beautiful girl came into this world
kicking and crying as if she wanted to go back, I was told
then with one look into her eyes, my heart was stolen in a strong
   hold
many years have passed now from that fateful day, my heart is
   still in her clutches of gold

HIDDEN SECRETS

the secrets of life are not known to anyone my friend
the hidden secrets of our creation are sure to remain hidden right
   to the end
don't waist your time and life searching for answers
to solve this puzzle, a new kind of man with a different kind of
   intelligence the almighty has to send

SHINING LIGHT

O' friend, I am bewildered and confused with this life
bewildered by time passing me by so quick and sorrow so rife
wherever I look, there are dark roads leading to nowhere
how a shining light would come in handy, like a hunter's knife

WORDS FROM THE HEART

so easy to run words on this little tongue
how they seamlessly flow like a stream of water or a rhyming
    song
some know the art of talking cheap, acting grand
lets decorate our personalities with words coming from the heart,
    all lifelong

FLIRTING WITH OBLIVION

when we are gone and hidden in the dirt
our dreams and desires are gone too, all in concert
all the sweat, despair and greed that followed us all along
are buried with us with oblivion to flirt

PUZZLES OF LIFE

out of nothing we came into being, a creature so refined
were given the gift of thought and understanding much of the
    universe, though ourselves confined
many great puzzles of life were solved by a few pounds of matter
    in our heads
pity the reason we are here and where we are going in the end,
    will remain undefined

FREEDOM

we are indeed prisoners of this earth, no escape
our feet on the ground and the eyes staring at the sky that covers
   us like a drape
but our thoughts can go far beyond the sky and the stars above
guess the only way for Man to fly and set himself free of confines
   of any shape

MESSAGE FROM THE OTHER SIDE

received a message in my mailbox from the other side
it said be joyous and cherish your life with pride
you have done all you could to live and let live
smile and make others smile as you go on this one-time ride

NEW WORLD

these little eyes see all the misery and suffering in this world
there are warm happy days in there too, but always followed by
    winter and cold
wish I could bring joy to everyone on this earth
remove the dark clouds of fear and set the world in a new mold

LOVE'S ATTRACTION

tomorrow the birds will be singing outside my door again
the flowers will dance in the gentle breeze behind my window
    pane
my love will be coming through those doors, her light shining
    through
all logic and wisdom are out of the window and all resistance to
    her attraction in vain

HOPE

let's be happy for a day with all the misery around
with sorrow and despair no solution is ever found
though the hearts ache and the eyes are teary
hope is a handy tool in your arsenal, its a shovel to upturn
  sorrows ground

MAN'S MOLD

saw the workshop of creation in a dream so scary and cold
in it, saw all creatures made from a pre-set mold
the only being not having a mold was Man himself
made me wonder if this is why his world is full of surprises ready
   to unfold

IGNORANCE

funny how those drowned in the sea of ignorance
do no struggle at all, total obedience
they are not aware of their drowning
they look happy and confident they go, nothing can be done but
   to watch in silence

PASSING LIFE

this life passed me by and I am still wondering
why did I come to this world and why do I have to go, keep
 pondering
there is no one who can give me the answer, this I know
give me another glass of wine, life is happier when I am
 slumbering

THE REALITY

dear God, you gave me this life and the bread I eat
happiness is all around me and the ones I meet
wine and joy for all, no worries, on clouds we sit
until I open my eyes and see the reality, things sure aren't that
    sweet

MAN OF GOD

man of God preaching the holy words to all
you think you have a strong connection to the almighty, looking
   tall
but all you say are hollow words
what will you do when the castles you build, under the weight of
   wisdom fall?

MY KIND OF GOD

when I am happy and well, life is good
God is a lovely friend of mine, always in the mood
when things turn nasty and lights are out for a while
life becomes meaningless at best, and God is a selfish ignorant
   entity shrouded in a black hood

UNDERSTANDING OF LIFE

the more I know about life, the more is left to know
the more I discover things, the more I feel I need to grow
seems like you're in a hole, the more you dig the deeper you bury
    yourself
this is Man's understanding of life in this one-time show

SILENT OBJECTORS

life is truly a stage and we are all the actors
all of us have a role to play in all kinds of sectors
the director is hidden from view, an imaginary entity
through time actors will reluctantly have to leave the stage one by
   one, all silent objectors

PURPOSE IN LIFE

what are you looking for in life?
how far do you want to reach, for what purpose is all your strife?
enjoy this little time you have and bring joy to all
once under the ground, idleness and boredom is damn rife

ALL CREATURES

we are indeed part of this earth as all other creatures
you can see signs of us in the fabric of galaxies, our signatures
however, so many of us think and act as if we own this place
with just a little wisdom in our heads, we'll see things clearly as
   figures in brightly colored pictures

FRIENDSHIP

O' how friendships make life worth living
fruits of friendship are joy and love and forgiving
let's remove all hatred and enmity from our hearts
for they produce the most bitter fruits of all, so pain giving

CREATION

indeed, we are all from the same pond of creation
different colors and shapes, but the same seed of life in all of us,
    and the same gift of imagination
why then some think they are different from others
when you turn the light of thought and wisdom off, you are on a
    journey of stagnation

MY OWN GOD

all my life I had the belief that I have a god walking alongside me
he protects me from harm and always watches over me, on the
    ground, in the air or in the sea
now that I am old, I see everyone, including my enemies, have a
    god of their own just like mine
finally became clear we all have gods of our own, nobody else can
    see

QUESTIONS FROM THE TEACHER

O' dear God, after all this time on earth I am still not sure what
   my objectives are?
If it was growth, physically or mentally, I guess I have grown as
   much as I could, though in a process so bizarre
but may I remind you that you are the teacher and me, like
   everyone else, your student
with all the questions in my head and the teacher never around,
   please don't expect me to shine like a star

DOWN UNDER

we are unruly guests for a few days in this place of wonder
appreciate this little time you have, for very soon we'll have to
   surrender
come and let's enjoy every minute of this precious life
when the last curtain falls, there is plenty of time to lay idle down
   under

BLUNDERS

came to this world and saw all its wonders

gained knowledge day by day, found the secrets behind all fires
and thunders

cloaked in arrogance when young, thought I knew a great deal
about this world and my creation

in the autumn of old age, found out I know nothing except my
awful blunders

ARROGANCE

arrogance is a terrible disease of the mind
you walk on this earth and feel everyone else should follow
    behind
just wait a little until you are old and frail
then you see yourself as a small pebble on the sea shore, left
    behind

JOY OF LIFE

when I was young, life was always a never-ending joy
day or night, warm or cold, they just added to the thrill of
    wanting to annoy
now when old, I still have the same thirst for life and its joy
this is the secret of being happy, treating life like a toy in the
    hands of a little boy

FOOD FOR THOUGHT

the food we eat truly becomes our mind and our emotions
it enables us to move our bodies and for our minds to travel the
  oceans
for some, what wonderful things that piece of bread can do
for others, it's just filth and darkness and mind's erosions

IN A DREAM

in a dream one night, I saw thousands of galaxies and stars
huge volcanoes and deep valleys on Jupiter and Mars
amazed and bewildered at this creation and the role of Man in it
wondered how this little Man can understand such vastness,
   though he himself is a tiny cog in the machinery of Gods

SPRING

hear the birds singing on the trees as spring has arrived
the nature has put on its best dress and all creatures are revived
flowers are dancing in the gentle breeze in harmony
a kiss on the lips of my love is just an expression of my joy,
   heartfully derived

POWER OF THOUGHT

ever wondered what sets us apart from other animals around us
if not for the power of thought, there is really no distinction
   between us
get on the ladder of thought and go up as far as you can
from afar you'll clearly see the true nature of all troubles that
   besiege us

IMMORTALITY

I live with the thought of immortality everyday, giving me hope
think that God will give me the life back again, once in a box and
   lowered into the ground by the rope
this is the dream Man lives by, albeit no evidence around
guess we keep on dreaming as it gives us a phony sense of relief,
   just like a dope

SPECK OF DUST

we all come to this life from nothingness
a speck of dust we were in the air, so small and meaningless
then we are alive for a few hours, always bewildered
in a blink of an eye, we disappear again into the world of
  emptiness

ULTIMATE SHOW

life is passing us by, whether we run or go slow
what is life but memories, good and bad in a row
no use fighting with the world, we will always be on the losing
  side
be happy with what destiny drops at your feet, God's ultimate
  show

LITTLE CHILD

little child of mine, take my hand and take me to the moon
throw a little smile at me and see my world become colorful soon
at your side there is no sorrow, I am light as a balloon
with you I feel wrapped in a cosy, heavenly cocoon

WHEN I AM GONE

when I am gone, nothing is left but memories
life ends for all, whether we are having fun or drowned in
   tragedies
all I have done remain as mental images for those who are left
   behind
then it doesn't matter if I had made millions of friends or enemies

DIFFERENT FACES

deep in thought, began wondering who am I?

so many faces are inside me, one for every occasion, some rowdy,
some shy

just maybe all conflicts within me are from these different faces I
carry

the wise in this world have one face, in and out, alas, they are in
short supply

BEING HUMAN

I make mistakes, that's what makes me a human
I do wrong and this is what you're suppose to do if you're a Man
God created us imperfect as all can see
sad part is when we go beyond our human nature and become
    inhuman

OUR WORLD

Man is truly sanity and insanity all wrapped into one
his world is also a reflection of his nature, bible in one hand, in
   the other the gun
as long as this is the routine, the world in the same way is spun
until Man changes his perspective on life, living will not be so
   much fun

LEFT IN THE COLD

all my life I ran after the material world
hasty and thirsty for more wealth, befriended anyone, young or
    old
until the big hand of destiny in later days grabbed me by the neck
then I saw in my haste I left all life behind, only to be left in the
    cold

MY WEDNESDAY

my beautiful Wednesday at last has come
the best day of the week, I am so ecstatic and some
it's all because you are here with me my love
truly the world changes on this day and a new man I become

SADNESS AND JOY

when you are sad inside, all your actions are grey and cold
you look at the world in black and white, all people around you
   become fuzzy, young and old
shake the sadness off your shoulders, be bold
color your world with happiness and joy, turn the dust of sorrow
   into gold

LITTLE MAN

our planet is nothing but a speck of dust amidst billions of stars
you don't see any sign of it from Jupiter or Mars
funny this little Man on earth feels so big inside, ruling over all
    other creatures
see how the cloud of arrogance disappears with one look into the
    sky and those shiny stars

OLD AGE

old age is no fun, all things seem to go in slow motion
sometimes your mind is still running fast, wants to swim the
    ocean
truly time waits for no one, a helpful word of caution
problem is when you're old your mind keeps drawing checks your
    body can't cash, a toxic potion

LAST DRAW

our last draw of the dice in life will come too soon
we are in the game for the last time, even if we're on the moon
make sure you are free of all attachments that may bog you down
it will be you alone on that last journey in your life's late
    afternoon

LIFE AT SIXTY

life at sixty, is it the beginning or the end?
you have lost a great deal of vitality, but your soul is on the mend
you feel young inside, still have arrows to bend
on the outside however, sadly your body is on a down hill trend

SHORT OF HEALTH

O' you who are hastily running after money and wealth
don't you know they will wrap around your neck, suffocating you
   in stealth
think a little about who you are and where you're heading at the
   end
there are many questions you need to find answers to,
   unfortunately you'll be short of health

TIME TO DESCEND

this life is all we have dear friend
hold it precious, we will lose it in the end
every breath is a diminishing gift given to us for free
once that last breath is taken, it's our time to descend

GIVING LIFE

although you are gone and have disappeared from view
my heart is with you and in there you are as good as new
when alone, my memories of you keep me warm and alive
funny, a living is kept alive by the one who has passed, who
   knew?

FACING MORTALITY

O' Man is full of trickery and vanity

day and night thinks of fooling others for his own gain, signs of
depravity

he thinks he is going to be around for good, having fun with false
sense of immortality

in a blink of an eye, he is wondering why his world fell apart,
facing oblivion and mortality

CHOOSING LAUGHTER

smile often and see the world smile with you
whether rich or in need, be happy and give joy to all others in
   view
life will pass us by whether we laugh or cry
choose laughter every time, the best gift given to only a few

OLD DRAGONS

when you see an old man, there is all weakness and fragility
take a look inside him if you can, some have dragons hidden
   there, no lovability
Man can easily hide his inside from view, be warned
a harmless kitten on the outside can well be a lion hiding inside,
   ready to pounce on vulnerability

SAME OLD SONG

we all know what is right and what is wrong
we all know when we are weak and when strong
but we keep on doing things that we know are bad and hurtful
it sure seems like we are all dancing to the same old song

THE REAL PERSON

truly no one knows what everyone else is about
we base our belief on what is on the outside, a look or a shout
how then can we know who someone really is?
as with horses, observe their behavior when at rest, and when
   they are taken for a long ride out

TRAVELLING MIND

even when I am imprisoned in a room
my mind is free to go wherever I wish, a flower ready to bloom
so why worry if you are physically limited
the power of thought can always lift you out of any darkness and
  gloom

DESTINY

drowned in the thought of why we are all left on our own
we are given life for no reason, the rest is unknown
the almighty has given us the power of will, some say
on the other hand, destiny grabs us by the neck, in its thunderous
   winds we are blown

HONESTY

O' how joyful life is when we are honest with all
no worries, no anxieties, always standing tall
no fear of any one or anything as nothing is hidden
people are happy and safe around honesty, no worries of a fall

TRANQUILITY

hours pass me by so quick and I get closer and closer to the end
if I could just live in the moment, life will be a heavenly trend
this life is sure hard and full of unpleasant surprises
my only weapon for survival is my thought, the only way for my
tranquility to extend

SHARING A SMILE

if you can not share your wealth with those in need
smile and share your happiness around, be a gardener sowing a
    seed
your laughter is contagious and will heal a great deal of pain
never be stingy with your smiles, no one will benefit from any
    kind of greed

OUR EARTH

this earth we call home, is our beloved mother
her equal kindness to all creatures is easy to discover
pity, we continue to destroy and damage this only place we have
the curse of future generations will sure come to us, as they
    continue to suffer

LIFE

life is analogous to a beautiful flower dancing in the breeze
it's fragrance all over the place, it endeavours to please
at some point it just seems like this glory will last for ever and
    ever
unbeknownst to all, a deadly storm is creeping closer with ease

WHEELS OF GREED

we are truly unaware of our own being and our life
since we are here, we take things for granted, acting like a sharp
    knife
think a little, slow down the wheels of greed and ever wanting
    more
very soon there comes that dreaded stop sign, it's you and a hell
    of a strife

WORLD OF A KING

see the King running his horses around
he thinks the world is at his feet, everyone on seeing him
   spellbound
with arrogance and vanity, he sets foot on the ground
nothing in his head but a fake reality, truth is sadly drowned

BOOK OF LIFE

read the book of life as many times as you like
the beginning and the end are always puzzling alike
we may just understand very little of the whole story, that's our
   limit
at the end we leave the book for others to read, despite their
   dislike

DOING FOR OTHERS

time is never enough in the arms of your love
no work is ever too much if it is for the good of the ones you love
the things you do only for self gain are lost in the passage of time
who you do things for will determine if you stoop low or stand
   above

SINKING SHIP

Man is separated from all other creatures because he can think
his footsteps are all over the earth and through time has
   discovered the missing link
one may wonder why then is his world full of misery and sorrow?
the answer just maybe he still needs to find his place on this ship,
   before it's ready to sink

LOOKING CLOSE

a wise man told me once, remember this life is too short
wake up from your stupor or dream of a sort
turn your eyes from afar and look closer to you
we are missing many things at our feet when we keep looking at
   the sky for support

LETTER TO GOD

O' dear God, listen to me if you can
why am I feeling down, what is your plan?
you keep many secrets from me on one hand, on the other, have
  made me the only intelligent being on this land
you see, something is truly a miss in your creation of this little
  Man

SHORTCOMINGS

Drink some wine and be joyful and gay
live your life to the full, work and play
we all have shortcomings and are bound to do wrong
stop counting faults of everyone else, see inside you and throw
   your own weeds away

OUR MOLD

we have been given wisdom, I am told
mixed with it, there is ignorance and greed making our mold
wisdom in most of us is sadly bound by the other two
that's why we are always stumbling in life, with nothing to hold

LIFE'S QUOTIENT

if I can only live in the moment
how wonderful life will be with no torment
indeed, life happens in the tiny fractions of time
one can find an ocean of happiness if he sees every second a life's
   quotient

BEING FREE

be self sufficient if you want to live free
depending on others for things you can do is work of a man on a
    foolish spree
once you get used to standing on your own feet
your heart is free and brave, no fear of anyone or any decree

BREATH

every single breath we take in any moment
becomes life and thought within us, rising us from being dormant
it is truly the essence of life itself
know its value, for it will be taken from all soon enough with
   great torment

TITLES

generosity is not giving a few when you have many
miser is not the one who gives little when all he has is a penny
we should be careful over the titles we give people
see the acts and not the words, as there are many so good at
  uttering words that lack substance of any

DESTINY AND US

whatever happened in the past is gone, throw it out in whole
   from your head, from the tip to the end
sorrow over what has already happened is not a smart way to
   mend
be calm and flow with the tide in this passing life
nothing was ever in your hands, destiny will make you straight or
   make you bend

GONE BUT NOT FORGOTTEN

saw you in a dream one lonely night
you are no more around, but your memory still lifts me up to the
    sky like a kite
you are gone and all beauty and excitement have left with you
wherever you are, know that your memory keeps me going, albeit
    a sad delight

PREACHERS

preachers of religions spending all their time worshipping their
own personal almighty
all of them think they are definitely on the right path, all other
words empty
never think that there may be other ways of understanding the
so-called God
they refuse to open other doors and peak inside, scared Satan
may knock on their doors, gently

MY OWN GOD

when I was young, I had one God who belonged to me and
   everyone else, and who gave us life
he gave me understanding of the world and courage to face any
   strife
as I got older that God of mine became small and smaller in
   stature
now at the end of my road, I see that God was indeed my own
   creation, the handle truly made the knife

MISSING THE PAST

there comes a day when you'll miss your past
that youth and vitality which went by so fast
your thoughts then become dark and all over the place, like a ship
   without a mast
accept whatever is thrown at you in this life, stay calm in your
   destiny's cast

TEMPORARY JOY

can never have enough of your beautiful face
your elegance makes me wonder just maybe you're not of the
   human race
to be near you is a gift this life has bestowed on me
pity this joy is only temporary, for we will be gone soon enough
   without any trace

YOUNG AND OLD

when I was very young, life seemed like a beautiful spring with a
   gentle breeze
so tranquil and tender my life was, everyone and everything
   seemed at ease
what was hidden from view was the storm brewing from afar
at this old age, now I see the storm approaching, destroying all
   beauty on its path, leaving sorrow and unease

POWER OF SMILE

have some fun the couple of days of life you'll be around
drink wine, dance and bring joy to all, make a sound
pointless carrying the heavy bag of sorrow on your shoulders
smile and see the joy in everyone else abound

SELFISHNESS

what we do for our own selfish needs will only last a short while
the cart you pull just for your own benefit may go just a mile
selfishness and greed are the roots of all problems with Man
although he knows soon he will end up as material which keeps
  lands fertile

MOTHER AND HER CHILD

asked a wise man which love is superior to all?
which love is as shiny as a diamond, always rising, never to fall?
he told me in a gentle voice, only one love stands on top of all
the love of a mother for a child, which is as grand as a mountain
   so wide and tall

THE HYPOCRITE

the hypocrite thinks he is fooling everyone for his own gain
in reality, he is deep in sorrow maintaining his reign
being one inside and out is the way to serenity indeed
O' what precious time is wasted by hypocrites, changing face
  masks with so much pain

THE INDISCRIMINATE SUN

if that glowing Sun could just utter a few words to Man
she would condemn him and humanity since time began
she would rightly claim that she has given warmth and light
   indiscriminately to all
then Man came along with his prejudice and greed as his survival
   plan

FINAL DESTINATION

do whatever you want, go wherever you like while you can
will never avoid that final destination, no matter where you ran
the one who builds mountains of wealth, and the one who has
　　nothing on earth
will both be hunted down by the same spear of destiny, all
　　according to plan

MAN'S PREDICAMENT

we are here for a day and gone the next
have seen it happen to others, have read it in the text
but we go on as if we are unaware of our predicament
when the time comes, we all look confused and badly vexed

OBSTACLES IN LIFE

destiny throws obstacles in our path as we go forward
we either jump over them or trip and sadly go downward
guess this is life, good and bad always in a mix
for some it's only goodness around, but for many the path of life
   is damn awkward

TRUE SELF

when alone, the things you gravitate towards display your true
    self
this is your real face, what you are made of, before they stood you
    on life's shelf
no matter how much you try to hide things in the open
in the journey of life, there are so many twists and turns that
    force you to be yourself

THE FOOL AND THE WISE

with the light of wisdom shining through all the crevices of the
mind
all darkness of prejudice and ignorance are removed, your
thoughts refined
look at the fool constantly falling as he keeps walking in the dark
he never looks for the light, so goes on in misery to which he is
fully resigned

NOT KNOWING

my life is almost gone and I am still unaware of my place in this
world
who brought me here and who is the one taking me away as I am
told?
my head is filled with memories of good and bad like everyone
else
don't know where I came from and where I am going, when I
leave my human mold?

SUPER HUMAN EXPERIMENT

became a fool one day and felt so proud and arrogant
forgot my real position in this world and felt as if everyone is my
    supplicant
then I had this terrible pain in my body that refused to go away
cried and begged every living and non-living entity for relief all
    night, forgot all about my super human experiment

KISS FROM AFAR

send you a kiss my love from far, far away
your memory still keeps all my sorrows at bay
how can I forget all our beautiful past, they are deeply embedded
   in my head
O' how I wish those memories could turn into reality today

DESTINY'S CARD

the almighty gave me life, though for just a few days
then I will disappear from view, become some memory, maybe
   from someone a praise
wish I could live in the moment as life is truly condensed in every
   drop of time
then life is a joy, and who cares what card destiny plays

TRAIN OF LIFE

sitting in the corner looking sad with those drooping eyes
you think the doors of the world are shut, to your surprise
remember you are riding this train of life just once
grab life by the neck and take it wherever you desire, before your
   demise

STRAW AND THE WAVE

life is analogous to a straw riding the waves
going up and down, not worried, going about its days
it is unaware of where it came from and where it is heading
in a blink of an eye it disappears from view, gone forever,
  becoming a tiny part of the waves

PRECIOUS TIME

my old man gently whispered into my ear before he passed away
life is a wind blowing through and you are a little straw on its way
you can fill your tummy with a piece of bread if you have to
beware of this precious time passing you by, before you are old
  with no room to sway

RAY OF LIGHT

O' my little one, say something to me
you have taken my heart and soul, all for free
when you are with me, I drown in your eyes and laughter
feels like you are a shining light, rays wrapped all around me, just
    no one else can see

BEING YOUNG

you see yourself a young man, big and strong, a big fish in a pond
you feel nothing can touch you, can say anything you want, make
  any sound
comes the night, you are incapable of defeating a tiny fly buzzing
  around your head
a paradox in Man's life indeed, a mind and a reality that fail to
  correspond

MEMORIES

O' dear brother of mine come again and hold my hand
take me to the valley of dreams, the one that looks so grand
pity, you are no longer around and your memories are the only
   thing left
will live with them throughout my life on this ever-changing land

OUR ACTIONS

the misery we are all drowned in
is nothing but our own actions and the tricks we spin
stop accusing others and the world for your troubles
be wise, otherwise the rope you hang on keeps getting thin

POWER OF HAPPINESS

my lonely heart be patient, there is no way out
a homeless has to survive under a bridge, that's what it's all about
this is a short life, smile through it if you can
happiness can light the way and magically remove any doubt

A WISH

wish I had just a little more patience
was a little less hasty in coming to conclusions, less complacence
swam like a fish on the waves of this life
had more understanding for the passing time, less negligence

DIFFERENT WORLD

all the sorrow we see in the world
is the result of ignorance of Man, young or old
if we could just see the benefit in everyone being happy
there will be a world even more beautiful than a shining gold

MESSAGE OF WISDOM

saw the eagle flying over the mountains
uttered a weird sound in the sky over the nature's fountains
felt it is giving me a message of wisdom from above
treasure life whether down on the ground or up on the mountains

SMILE

stand up and give me a big smile
your face will look much prettier smiling, by a mile
the ugly and the bad of the world are truly for every one
let all that go and dance your sorrows away, give life a new trial

LIFE IN VAIN

I am afraid of my time running out, my efforts in vain
no time left to correct my mistakes or jump onto the right train
I know as the end nears, regret and remorse are useless tools
strange I know all this, but keep on going along in pain

THE MASTER

told myself one day, stop waiting for the world to turn your way
you are a tiny cog of intelligence in this machinery any way
the world turns the way it's meant to, to your dismay
create your own world the way you want, then make it turn as if
   you're the master of the play

LIVING IN THE MOMENT

never worry about two things in life
the thing which has passed you by and the thing which is still to
    color your life
live in the moment as that is the only time happiness is rife
then you'll be joyful and will pass on happiness to all around you
    in life

DRIVEN BY MOTIVE

how we humans are all driven by a thing called motive
want to be respected, to be loved, free of all thoughts that are
    corrosive
but sadly, we constantly fail in achieving the things we aspire to
just maybe we should stop searching for them outside, going
    through a therapy that is implosive

CHANGING COLORS

you color the world just the way you are colored inside
can never get away from this, there is no where to hide
start a new paint job within you, colorful as spring
then see everything change around you, darkness moving to the
  wayside

TRIGGERS OF HAPPINESS

hearing the birds sing in the morning
all sadness is washed away by that magical sound behind the
   awning
just think how easy one can change moods, if he lets the vibes in
it is such simple triggers that take us to a happier times from the
   depth of mourning

TROUBLED MAN

nothing is more satisfying than making a troubled Man happy
nothing is as degrading as bringing more sadness to the one who
    is needy
why then there is so much sorrow around us in the world
we are all so busy running for more, blind to the desperate child
    scouring the dirt for a single penny

FINAL FALL

hear the tick-tick of the clock hanging on the wall
it is warning you of the passage of time and getting close to when
   the curtains fall
alas, we ignore the warnings and carry on with our own mundane
   things
until it is too late, the alarm rings and we are set for that final fall

DROWNED

O' you beautiful girl, sit beside me for a while
I am an earthen floor and you cover me like a precious tile
what can I say to you when you hold me spellbound?
I lose myself in your elegance and drown helplessly in that
   magical smile

STUMBLING MAN

finding faults in others is easy my friend
as long as you think you have no faults of your own to mend
we all keep looking out for some one else to make a mistake
that's why we are always stumbling and falling, never able to
   ascend

BUILDING WISELY

the wise always builds, new structures full of life and grace
he doesn't care what everyone else says, he is into putting a smile
    on a face
a fool on the other hand does everything for his own good
he also builds structures, but dark and hollow no one can ever
    embrace

PASSING LIFE

autumn leaves dropping onto the ground
is a sign of sorrow and separation so profound
the poor and the rich of the world can hear this same message in
    a clear sound
this is a passing life which ultimately ends in a fall, from which
    there is no rebound

FINAL STATEMENT

opened my eyes to this world with amazement
went through the early stages of life trying to learn, relentless
    engagement
then the mid-life came and along with it suspicions and lots of
    painful unanswered questions
now on the final lap, guess no more struggles left, quietly
    surrendered to my fate, a sad final statement

FATHER AND SON

my father held my hand just before he passed away
whispered gently with closed eyes as if he was dreaming away
this is life my son beware, just a few more days and you'll be in
   my place
live so there are no regrets when it comes to your turn whispering
   away

MOVING THE WORLD

life is filled with times of joy and sadness
it is filled with acts of sanity and madness
just keep looking on the bright side of things and dispel darkness
remember you can move the world with one act of kindness

THE DIFFERENCE

saw a poor fallen man in need of a helping hand
people passing by as if he was invisible, unworthy, a desert of a
   land
thought to myself isn't he indeed part of us all with that same
   DNA strand?
what makes us different from one another then, one day I hope to
   understand

MAN AND GOD

drowned in my thoughts I began to wonder
is Man a creation of God or is it the reverse, the thought struck
    me like thunder
then I was fascinated by the thought of this little Man creating
    that giant God up in the heavens
just to constantly beg him for forgiveness and be scared of his
    punishments after he goes under

CHANGE THROUGH TIME

the wind of change blows incessantly all over the place
it touches all of us, all nature with its own kind of grace
the message is one thing, everything will change through time
Man is the only creature being pulled through the change kicking
  and screaming in disgrace

MAN AND THE STARS

look up into the sky at night
see all the stars shining bright
all dancing in harmony and blinking at us from above
pity, Man is down here getting ready for his next fight

ONE TIME RIDE

the river of humanity flows along with no hesitation
we are all part of it, whether in a willing or forced participation
we are all aware this is a one time ride
let's relax and enjoy the trip as much as we can, let's stop all that
   condemnation

RADIATING BEAUTY

as the flower wilts away one day
our life is set to end, all to our dismay
the flower radiates beauty all through its life
this is what Man is supposed to do, without going astray

THE WOODEN FRAME

always running after money and fame
always wanting more, nothing is ever enough, always looking for
    someone to blame
this is the story of Man on his journey of life
then he is caught badly surprised when his little time runs out,
    resting quietly in a wooden frame

THE RIGHT TIME

do the right thing while you are able and free
our strength will not last forever, look around you, you'll see
when old and fragile you can't do much, even if you want to
there is no use in building a hive, without a bee

GIFTS OF LIFE

woke up and saw the beautiful Sun smiling at me
as if she wanted me to get out, jump around or climb a tree
radiating light and life equally to all, expecting nothing back
the least I can do is enjoy these gifts of life, hoping others can see

MAKING MY OWN PLAY

two intriguing days in my life, the day I was born and the day I'll
  pass away
for both I am just a passenger with nothing to say
the time between the two is when my life actually happens
maybe the only time I can take hold of the steering wheel and
  make my own play

FRIEND OR A FOE

destiny can be a friend or a foe
all depends on what we do on the road of life as we go
for the one who just sees himself and nobody else
destiny is a dark alleyway full of nasty potholes, giving you pain
  from head to toe

TAINTED WORLD

these eyes are my windows to the world
when I am sad all is tainted, dark, tired and old
O' friend pour me a glass of wine, so I can forget all and bring
  back the joy
with it I'll wash away the taint, once again my world becomes as
  shiny as gold

STRANGE LIFE

life is mighty strange as they say
you come into it from oblivion, not having a say
once here, you do everything in your power just to stay
but soon without your consent, that life ends and you're back to
  dust again, all to your dismay

TO MY SON

go along my son, tease life as much as you like
be wild, throw stones at death, tell it to take a hike
this is your time to make your mark on this land
to live as you want, create and be godlike

REACHING THE MOUNTAIN TOP

never let anyone tell you what to do
you have the power to split atoms in two
all you have to do is be wise and think things through
then you'll reach mountain tops only touched by a few

NEVER TOO LATE

never too late for a kiss or an embrace
never too late to tell your loved ones they are impossible to
    replace
never too late to give a helping hand to the one fallen out of grace
never too late to pick yourself up from any shame or disgrace

TREE OF LIFE

what really makes me different from you are my actions
the way I look or the color of my skin are all superficial
    abstractions
let's see the reality of who we are in this life for once
we are all tiny leaves on a single tree of life, to be shed after a
    short time of absurd interactions

BLUE SKY

blue sky was smiling at me just the other day
as if bragging about its beauty and engaging in a foreplay
imagined in my head a beautiful woman is extending her arms
    for an embrace
it's nature giving us love and affection in its own way

RIVER OF LIFE

sitting by the river seeing the water flow
a reminder of how life is passing us by, often fast, sometimes slow
the river is constantly moving, taking everything along, replacing
the old with the new
life is constant movement too, as the light of the old fades away
into oblivion, new ones start to glow

www.ingramcontent.com/pod-product-compliance
Lightning Source LLC
Chambersburg PA
CBHW070444090426
42735CB00012B/2456